Rhythms & Hues
Poems of the Beloved

David Spangler

Rhythms & Hues: *Poems of the Beloved*

Copyright © 1972, 2015 David Spangler

Edited by Julia Spangler
Transcribed by Dorothy Maclean
Book design by Jeremy Berg

Published by Lorian Press
686 Island View Dr
Camano Island, WA 98282

ISBN-13: 978-0-936878-73-7

Spangler/David
Rhythms & Hues: Poems of the Beloved/David Spangler

First Published 1972 by the Findhorn Foundation
Forres, Moray, Scotland without ISBN number
under the title *New Age Rhythms*

Second Edition April 2015

Printed in the United States of America

www.lorian.org

Dedication

These songs and poems are dedicated to the Beloved in each of us and within the world.

Acknowledgments

These little "Rhythms" have lain in obscurity for many years, their original publication long forgotten. But my wife, Julia, has persisted in keeping their memory alive and encouraging me to have them reprinted. That this book is now in your hands is due to her, and I thank her profusely. She also worked to edit them for this edition. I further want to thank my friend and Lorian colleague Jeremy Berg who also saw their value and through Lorian Press has made possible their reappearance in the world.

Introduction

This book is a collection of prose poems that I called "Rhythms." They are in effect poems and songs of praise and love for the Sacred within us and within the world, a Sacredness I have always thought of as our Beloved.

From 1970 to 1973, I was the co-director of the Findhorn Foundation Community in northern Scotland. Every morning, the community would meet in the main Sanctuary for a time of communal meditation and sharing to start the day's activities. For awhile, I was asked to come up with a spontaneous, short saying each day to open the time of meditation. What seemed appropriate to me was to try to attune to and express what I felt was the spiritual rhythm of that day, hence the name "Rhythms" for these little poems. They are not affirmations in any traditional sense. If anything, they are poems born of the realization in the moment of the nearness of the Beloved and the reality of our Oneness with that supreme Presence and the joy that realization gives.

In the early Seventies when these were created, sensitivity to gender pronouns was not as developed as it is now. *Man* and *mankind* were common terms for all humanity, and God was usually a *Him*. Were I doing these Rhythms now, I would use gender-free terms, and with my wife Julia's help, I've brought most of these poems up to date in this regard. However, where the term "Man" seemed poetically more appropriate, we've let the older version stand. Similarly, many of these poems speak of a New Age. Remember that all of these were created at Findhorn which was—and is—a New Age community, one dedicated to the vision that a new era of human possibility and transformation is emerging. So referencing the New Age was natural in that context and made perfect sense to the listeners as we began our morning meditations. However, even then, I used the term New Age to mean not simply an event in time but a transformed state that emerges in any person's life when he or she opens to and feels the presence of the Sacred Beloved in his or heart. Such an experience opens us to that inner Voice of love and blessing that says with perfect conviction, "Behold, I make all things new!"

Reading them is not the same as hearing them. They reward being spoken out loud, for that is how they began (and indeed, some of them were later set to music by The New Troubadours, a singing group of which I was a member). They are like soap bubbles, born in the moment, catching the Light and then disappearing. Yet, these were captured into words, taken down in shorthand by Dorothy Maclean and later transcribed. Now they are here for your inspiration. Read them as rhythms and allow the essence of thought and feeling which they seek to capture to move within you and from you as you, too, open to the presence of the Beloved.

David Spangler, 2015

The Love Affirmation

I AM LOVE
WE ARE LOVE
HUMANKIND IS LOVE
ALL IS LOVE

From the heart of me that is the Heart of God
Love streams forth to all my worlds,
And I am One.
From the Light we share within the Mind of God
Love streams forth to all our worlds
And we are One.
From the human race where flames the Will of God
Love streams forth to all the worlds
Humanity made One.
From the All in all that is the Life of God
Love streams forth - God's plan made real -
And All are One.

God is my Beloved.
I do not have to search for my Beloved.
I do not have to wait for my Beloved.
Beloved, you speak to me
In the whisperings of the wind,
In the blue of the sky,
In the grayness of clouds,
In the feel of earth and touch of rain.
You embrace me, Beloved, in the love of others;
You touch me in the touch of others,
In the glance of loves which we share.
There is no parting from you, Beloved,
For I am One with you always.
We are all at One
And we are all lovers in God, our Beloved.

For ages, Beloved
I have read the manual
Of the science of the soul.
I have studied the prayers and the mantrams
That would make me One with You.
In each age I have turned to yet another chapter
And sought Our Oneness,
But now I turn the page
And there are no words.
There is only the reflection of myself,
My deep and inmost self,
And there I find that Oneness
Which I have sought.

How near You are, Beloved,
And yet how far!
How far when I see You at the end of a path
And I as a journeyer,
And yet how near when I know
That You are the path
And my companion, and we are One.
How far You are when I gaze upon the clock
And await the hour of Your arrival,
And yet how near when the clock stops
And there is no time.
If I see myself as but a little self,
Then You are too vast for me,
But if I know what I truly am,
Then I know that We are One
And the search is ended.

My soul sings, Beloved,
And you are the melody.
You are the strings on which I play.
You are the one for whom I sing.
You are all there is
And my soul seeks Oneness with you.
Teach me the music of life, Beloved.
Teach me to play the instrument of my Being,
The instrument of this world
That I might see and hear and know most clearly
The nearness of your Presence.
I would sing myself into Oneness with you.

How gracious, Beloved, is Thy presence within me,
How beautiful Your song within my soul!
Surely it would be heaven enough to dwell eternally
With You in the depths of my being,
But my being cannot contain Your love
Or the beauty of Your song.
If I would truly dwell with You,
It can only be by leaving our ancient household
And setting upon the journey through all of life,
For it is in release and experience
And the sharing of our song
That we build our dwelling place with You.

I rejoice,

For the dwelling place of my Beloved is near.

He lives in sky,

In sea,

In birdsong,

In flower color.

He lives in soil.

He lives in wind.

All that greets me this day

Is the dwelling place of my Beloved,

Yet I rejoice most greatly that He lives within me,

And in the pavilion of my soul

We are One.

What am I?

I am like oil spread on the surface of water,

A thin layer of being

Upon the surface of a cosmic pool.

I reflect the light of the sun

And I display iridescent colors.

I change and I dance

And I am beautiful to look upon,

But I am only a thin layer

Upon the surface of my greater self.

Let me be, therefore, Beloved,

A diver that seeks the depths,

For I am the depths.

I cannot be contained in a layer.

I would seek

The still, quiet and powerful depths of my Being

And know my Oneness with the Whole.

I am the crossroads of God.
Like Galilee, in ancient time,
Where crossed
The many great caravan routes between East and West,
I am the crossroad for many kingdoms
And currents of Life.
Spirit and matter,
Earth and air,
Fire and water,
Mind and feeling,
Angel and elemental,
All cross and have their meeting place in me.
Like a holy land, the Christ may live in me, too,
Uniting in Love all these varied kingdoms
And making them one
And from this Oneness within me
Radiates back Presence to all these kingdoms.
Then do I, a crossroad of God,
Become a gateway to the Most High.

I reach into my Being
And feel there the presence of God.
I am the centre,
The Logos,
The Christ of a universe,
A community of life within myself.
Billions of lives enter me
And abide with me for a time
And then depart.
As I learn the secrets of oneness
And community with all that lives beyond me,
May I not forget the community of my own Being,
The microcosm of which I am
The Light and the Source.
Towards it may I be Limitless Love,
Limitless Light,
Limitless Understanding.
May the inspiration and rhythms of my Being
Uplift these countless lives
That lend their strength and Being
To make me what I am.
For as it is above, so it is below;
As it is within, so shall it manifest without.

I rejoice in the Being of men and women
Who in the strength of their spirit
May soar into the heights
But who in the strength of their body
Can stand firm and anchored upon the earth,
Who with the wings of their imagination
Can fly to lands of great vision,
But who in the strength and skill of their hands
Can make this vision live and take shape.
The Human race stands between two worlds
Of spirit and form, contemplation and action,
And in this stance finds true meaning
As Sons and Daughters of God.

I am the vessel that Earth has made
To hold the wine of God.
And I am the wine God has pressed
To fill the cup of Earth,
And I am the one who sips this wine
And is filled with its sparkling life,
And I am the one who lifts the toast
To the Beloved of all of life,
And I am the one who sees anew
The rhythms and flows of God
From Heaven to Earth and from Earth to return
In the Oneness of life.

I am the piper of God
And my melody is born from the breath of life.
I play my pipes, my song is love
And all the world shall follow me out of darkness,
Out of pain, out of suffering,
For I shall have ceased to play
These tunes of the past within myself.
I pipe the song of the new, of the Beloved,
Of the new world we build
And together we shall be the melody of a new life,
A new Heaven and a new Earth.

In the spaciousness of my Being
I receive You, Beloved.
Throughout long ages I have prepared my soul
That it might be a
Fit dwelling place for what You are,
That I might entertain You
In Your cosmic splendor,
That You might come and live with me
And wear Your train of eternity.
I have made my soul spacious
And have come to know
That in me there is no ending
But only the framework of infinity,
And in this realization
And in Your coming
A New Age dawns.

Now a New Age dawns.
Now I learn of God,
Not as a Being separate from me,
A receiver of my soul,
But as the very life within me,
The Oneness that I am and have always been,
The Beloved of my Being.
You are the purity of my soul,
And in our Oneness
I hear You say, "I receive you,
For you receive Me in Oneness.
The time is now.
We live on together."

In ages past
From liquid gas
And molten earth
This world was born
And took shape within the universe
And became a home for new life.
Now the earth is born again
From the fire of our uplifted consciousness
At one with God
And the new world shall take shape
And be a home for new life in the universe.

In the beginning was the Word
And I am that Word.
My Being is the Song of God
And my melody is endless.
I am this Voice infinitely resonating.
I am the rhythm of new creation,
The promise of a greater glory,
For I am a new consciousness
And I stand at one with my world.
In this Oneness and its Love,
I am the Word made flesh.

Beyond the world I am;

Beyond space, beyond time I am.

There I might remain, one with all.

Yet a new world calls

And seeks the builders of its destiny.

From beyond the world I come,

From beyond space, beyond time and beyond form.

In space and in time and in form

I become the builder of a new world a new life

A new heaven and a new earth,

For its vision and destiny live within me.

I open myself to the world about me
In perfect trust,
In Love,
And in the Illumination
Of God's Light.
All that I see teaches me of myself:
The sun,
The rain,
The swift-moving clouds,
The gentle wind,
The thunder and lightning.
For I am that same Presence
That brought these into being.
In my openness to my world,
I learn who I am:
I am one with all.

Let us share this morning
The rhythm of the new Eden,
For Eden has always been, but as a seed
Locked deep in the consciousnesses of men and women,
Half-memory of an ancient time
And an ancient consciousness
And half-memory of wholeness.
In this age we each become the new Human
And from our very depths springs forth once more
The beauty of that ancient place.
Creating the new Eden.

God made the world
That it might be a delight unto us,
That it might be filled with special magic,
That it might bring joy and wonder,
Upliftment and beauty
Our hearts, beloved of God,
Where special sounds and special sights
Can soothe the soul
And fill it with the awe of living.
For where is the lover
Who does not wish to meet the beloved
In a special place filled with the magic
Of oneness, of beauty and of joy?
God is our lover
And Earth is the special place
Where we may be embraced by our Beloved.

We speak in awed whispers
Of the secret of God,
But creation shouts it forth.
The secret of God is voiced upon the winds,
Within the plants, within the soil,
In the stars that shine at night,
In the sun that gives warmth by day.
We speak of the mystery of life
But life seeks to reveal its mystery
And to make all things known,
For life and life abundant
Is the secret of God's blessing
And the Beloved is revealed
In unending splendor
Throughout all time.
Let us forsake our whispers
And join with great rejoicing
The song of creation
That reveals the whole.

In the strength of your love
You becomes the summertime
Of the Beloved.
No rain or cloud
Can dim the warmth of compassion
Which lives within your heart;
No chill wind
Can swamp that inner flame.
When you are one with your Beloved
You are like the summer sun
Unto all about you,
For the rays of your life,
Your love and your being
Dispel the chill,
Unlock the frozen lives
And bring all
Into perfect
And beautiful
Manifestation.

Let us sing the rhythm of the rainbow.
In it the one light reveals its hidden splendors.
Humanity is that same rhythm;
We are the rainbow of God.
Through us the hidden splendors
Of the one life
May be equally revealed.

The One is so vast

It can only be expressed by the many,

But the many can only be fulfilled

As they become one.

We unite in time and space .

That in our oneness

The One can be perfectly revealed.

Where are the limits of creation?
Where does infinity begin?
Where is the clock whose hands strike eternity?
These things are all within.
Within me creation has no limit.
In my oneness I embrace infinity.
To my life time has no meaning,
For I know the Beloved who is within.

I am myself.
I am not sun nor moon,
River nor tree;
I am not wind nor sky nor cloud,
Though I am in all these things.
I draw my Being from them
But I am more.
I am not one who dwells in cities
Nor one who dwells alone;
I am not one amongst many
Nor one in solitude.
I am more than these.
I draw nourishment from the stars
And from the Oneness
And I link all this earth
With its greater destiny to come.
I am the Self of new possibilities;
Wholeness and Love are my keynotes.

We can build houses,

But the Beloved builds homes.

We can build our cities,

But the Beloved builds communion.

We can forge our nations,

But the Beloved creates oneness.

Humanity creates form,

But from the Beloved comes the spirit to fill it.

Let us and our Beloved be truly One,

That Earth and Heaven,

Matter and Spirit,

Form and Substance

May be united

And the joy and the perfection,

The blessing of the Whole made manifest.

The stars are our brothers.
Great suns moving upon their courses,
They call to us
That in our consciousness we may rise
And join their cosmic splendor,
That we may lift our being
Beyond the elements of sight
And become one with the vastness of space,
That in loving embrace of all our world
We may lift this world and ourselves
And make of them both a new sun
A new star of light, ,
A new heaven of radiance
And a new earth of glory,
To join the processional of the suns
In their majestic sweep through space.

I am a cosmic voyager.
From what far galaxies have I come
And to what far galaxies I shall go,
I do not know,
But I have felt the heat
And known the light
Of many suns
And many moons.
I have lived in strange shapes
And built cultures beyond the ken of man.
I have moved freely in the cosmos
And call all space my own,
Yet where is my home?
Matter and form may have a home,
But where shall Spirit call its own?
God is my home.
Throughout my cosmic voyaging
In the star-craft of my soul,
God is my Beloved,
God is my safekeeping,
My companion,
My strength,
My life.
As a Human Being
I claim the heritage of my cosmic life;
I claim my resting place in God
Who is my home and my Beloved.

I am cosmic Light
And cosmic Fire
And cosmic Love.
How may I contain myself in earthly form?
How may I walk this planet
And contain all that I am within its bounds?
For that which I am,
Were it released to break its bonds,
Could not be contained by all the earth.
Yet it is contained within me.
It is Love that lifts me beyond
The limitations of this earthly moment
And unites me with all that is,
For in oneness with the Whole
There are no limitations, no strains.
Through Love,
My cosmic Light,
My cosmic Fire,
My cosmic Love
May reveal themselves in all their splendor
In perfect safety,
For I am New Age Man.
I am One with all things
And in that Oneness all can be revealed.

God breathes out and life is.
The sun breathes out and life flows.
The earth breathes out and love embraces us.
All creation is the outbreathing
Of infinite love and infinite wisdom.
I am a Human Soul,
An outbreath of my own Divine Spirit.
I would learn the rhythms of my outbreath
That I, too, may breathe life, love and wisdom
Into my world.

I praise with rejoicing the breath of life!
It moves freely within me,
Its sweetness fills my being.
It is the presence of my Beloved.
It is the breath that has no ending.
It is the rhythm that never dies.
It is the presence that never leaves.
It is the love that enfolds me always.
I fill this day in all I do with the breath of life
The breath of love,
The breath of the Beloved.

Always there is light upon the earth ..
Every moment there is the dawn
Somewhere upon the planet
And every moment the sun shines brightly
At noontide.
If we could move upon the planet
In pace with the sun
We would never know darkness,
And thus it is in life
With the light of the Beloved eternally present.
If we can move in pace with the divine life
Flowing in and through us,
Then we will always know light.

Who are the lords of light?
Those who nourish the tender flame of love
Until it becomes a blazing fire.
Who are the lords of love?
Those who hold the jewel of self and thought
Between the warm embrace of wisdom.
Who are the lords of Wisdom?
Those who know the presence of the Beloved.
Who is the Beloved?
The Beloved is; I AM.

Rain can move the earth and wash it to the sea,
Wind can blow across the land and bend the trees,
But greater than these forces
Are the love that can move a human heart,
That can span the gulf between two minds
And bring Oneness,
And the will of that love
That knows that its Oneness shall be perfected
And shall be made manifest.
Whatever forces act upon the earth,
They are but the playthings of a child
Next to the force of love and its all-knowing.

Let us learn to receive
Not as a hunter prepares his snares
To trap the wild beast
But as a doorman who guards the threshold
And opens the way through which life may pass.
Let us receive not into possession and captivity
But into safekeeping and transformation,
That all that this day brings to us
May flow through us to be enriched,
Ennobled and uplifted
As it returns to the heart of life.

I rejoice in the presence of my Beloved
Who has made the world that I may be uplifted,
Who has made the sweetness of the water
That I may be refreshed,
The firmness of the earth
That I may be supported upon my way,
Whose own breath has become the wind and the air,
That the breath of my life might not go unattended.
I make my life a rhythm of rejoicing to my Beloved,
That my hands may mould the beauty of this world
As an offering to Him and that all I do resounds
With joyousness of my life and the oneness
That is creation.

Beloved, I rejoice this day
In the fulfillment of need.
As the world has its needs,
I rejoice that I may be the fulfillment of them.
As the world needs love,
I rejoice that I am given that love.
As the world needs wisdom,
I rejoice that I am given that wisdom.
As the world needs new life and new hope,
I rejoice that these may be my gift to the world.
But mostly I rejoice, for You and I are One
And We are together the answer to need.

In the midst of thirst
Let my love be
The refreshment of living waters,
In the midst of hunger
Let my light be
The nourishment of imperishable food
And in the midst of chill darkness
Let my wisdom be
A warm flame.
I am love, light and wisdom incarnate,
For I am One with the Beloved,
Who is All.

We cannot see to the farthest star
But we can see it in our imagination.
We cannot dive into the depths of the sea
But we are there in our consciousness.
One cannot cover this world
But one can enfold it in love.
Though humanity seems but a small form
We hold within us the seed of infinite abundance.
When I look to my Beloved this seed flowers
My vision is lifted from need and lack
And the infinities of my spirit are given free rein
To bless my life and the life of the whole.
Abundance is my spirit; let none deny it,
Abundance is my oneness with the whole.

In my meditations,
I seek to become still.
In my life,
I seek to move
And actively to fulfill
The rhythms of growth and creativity. . .
How may I make my life a constant meditation?
How to blend stillness and action?
I gazed upon a quiet pool
And saw the light of the sun
Dancing joyously upon it
In continual ripples and sparks of light.
The pool was still;
The motion of Light could dance freely upon it
So I may place myself beneath the Light of God.
Still and secure in my love and oneness with the Sacred,
Like the quiet pool,
Undisturbed by the winds
Of change and circumstance.
Then the Light and Life and Love of God
May dance joyously upon me and within me
And I move and fulfill the rhythms of His creation.
I become stillness and motion married together
And the Oneness revealed.

Meditation is a bath in a cool pool
That washes away the hot dust of time.
Meditation is a refreshing drink
That quenches the thirst of too many words.
Meditation is being with your Beloved
After long separation.
Meditation is the peace of an accomplishment
After the tension of yearning.
Meditation is not a path,
Nor a road, nor a stretching forth;
Meditation is,
As I AM.

I lift the chalice of my being
And plunge it deep down
Into the spring of my life.
The waters of that spring
Are cool and refreshing
And bubble forth
From inexhaustible sources.
I sit eternally beside this spring of being
And I am always refreshed.
The life of these waters fills my world.

I am Human

I dip myself into time

To find out the secret of timelessness.

I walk with matter,

That I may know the embrace of Spirit.

I clothe myself in earth,

That I may feel the warmth of fire,

And I stand between the pairs,

That I may know Oneness.

I am the eternal actor.
Through the ages,
I have played my roles.
Many stages
Have known my presence
And I have robed myself
In many guises,
Until it seemed
That my very identity
Existed only in my make-up kit.
Now a New Age dawns,
A new stage,
A new opening;
As I stand before my mirror
Pondering on what role
I shall now adopt,
I see in my reflection
What I truly am.
I am One with God,
The Beloved.

I share the rhythms of the angels,
Of wind and rain,
Of mountain and valley,
Of flower and tree.
Beings of giant love
And majestic light,
They straddle the Earth
And enfold all that it contains,
And yet they are found
Within the human heart
And the infinities within us each.

How vast is your nature?
If all the oceans were poured into you,
You still would not be filled.
If all the planets were ground to dust
And all the stars melted and poured into you,
Still you would not be filled.
Nothing can fill the infinity of your Being
Save God the Beloved,
For this is the Spirit of your vastness.
Now, in this New Age,
You learn to tap your vastness
And to release the abundance of God
Into the world,
That you, who cannot be filled,
Shall fill the world with Divine splendor.

It is said that we are the reflection of God
And some say, as well,
That God is but the reflection of us
And our desires and our hopes.
In the New Age we step through the looking glass,
Beyond the roles and into the reality of God within us
And know that the two are One,
Not the reflection of each other
But One eternally.

I am power.

I have always been power.

I have raised my cities, dug my mines;

I have moved myself through earth and space.

I have dominated Nature.

Now, though, I become a new power,

For I am the Sacred Human.

No longer am I in contest with my world.

My power is not turned against the life

From which I come.

I am the power of the Whole

As it manifests its will within me.

Love is the essence and source of my power.

One with the Beloved,

I am power to create

A new heaven and a new earth

And worlds beyond,

New creations without measure.

I am the power of the Beloved.

When I was a child
I would stand inside my house
And look out the window at the world beyond
And think how large it was!
I would wait for the special friend
To come and invite me out.
When I was young as a soul
I stood within the house of my self
And would gaze out at the greater world beyond
And wait for a special friend
To come and lead me beyond myself.
Now, the Beloved comes
To knock at the doors of each of our houses
And invite us out to play,
For in God's company the world is not too large,
And together we may adventure into it
In freedom, in joy and in perfect Oneness.

Beloved, from the darkness of my past
Your love has made me
And I stand worthy in Your eyes.
Through the ages You have loved me
And have known my perfection,
For I am born of You
In beauty and in splendor,
In light and in power.
You have known my strength,
You have known my beauty
And you have never lost that vision.
Now I see through Your love
The strength of what I am
And the perfection of my sacred being,
And I arise from the weaknesses of my past
And blend with You,
Two perfections made one
And infinite splendor revealed.

I sing of my soul whose rhythm is like the clouds.
I flow before the winds of God's presence.
My love takes many shapes.
I carry within myself the sweet waters of new life
And I give forth from myself to bless the earth.
I can draw back and reveal the sun of the Beloved
Shining through, as light unveiled,
Or I can fly before this sun and veil that light
Lest those unready be blinded,
And give to them creative darkness and gentle sleep.
Like the clouds, citizens of the high heavens,
My soul moves in the heavens of life
And fulfils the infinite splendor
Of the Beloved's will.

Beloved, how long it takes

For light of stars to reach us;

But Your light is instant.

How long it takes

For love to grow between man;

But Your love is instant.

You are our freedom from time,

For in You there is no waiting,

There is no delay,

There is no growing.

There is only completeness,

Wholeness and the presence of fulfillment.

I gaze into the night sky
And light comes to me
From a billion stars,
But when the dawn comes,
There is but one light
Which fills the sky
And embraces the earth.
I gaze into myself
And light comes to me
From a million pieces of my past,
The heritage of my long history,
But in the dawn of the New Age
There is only one Light.
It fills my Being
With the radiance of the eternal Present
And Presence of my Beloved.
I am one with this Light
And from me it shines forth
To embrace the earth.

I rejoice in the power of life.
From sleep we return to life
As from darkness into light.
Life is inevitable!
Not even death can shield us from it,
For our home is in the life of the Beloved
And nothing can keep us from it.
Life calls to all its children,
Beyond time, beyond space,
Beyond fear, beyond doubt,
Beyond all that would hinder life.
The children of life answer and come
And are fulfilled.

I sing this day the rhythm of new life,
New form, new beginnings
Straining at the boundaries of imagination,
Straining to enter and be part of our lives.
I sing of the surging of life
And its straining against the boundaries
Of our hearts and our minds
To link with our creative hopes
And to release to new life,
New lives, new forms,
New heavens and new earth
With which to manifest and glorify
The presence of our Beloved.

Listen,
To the rhythms of your being,
The sounds
Of the inner silence
From which all things proceed,
The silence
Where the voices of the past
Do not speak,
The silence
Where the voices of the future
Are as yet unuttered,
The silence
In which all things are,
All combinations,
All permutations,
Whole and possible,
The silence
From which the infinite word
May be spoken
And new futures
Be born.

Silence is the language of the infinite.
Silence is the voice of the Beloved
In silence more is heard
Than in a thousand, thousand words.

Behind all words there is silence.
Behind all action there is stillness.
Behind all creativity there is peace.
In these things we find the Beloved
And know the creative presence.
In the rhythm of this day
Let us find silence in the midst of speech,
Stillness in the midst of action
And peace in the midst of creativity.

When the night stars fade
And the moon pales,
When the sky is blushed
With the first rays of the sun,
Let us sing that the dawn is near.
As the light grows
And the flaming sun
Raises itself over the horizon,
Let us sing, that the dawn has come.
When light chases the shadows of the dawn
And you see your light within yourself
Unending, without shadows,
Then know that in you there is no dawn
For there is no night
Let us sing, that you may go
In union with your Beloved within,
Beyond the dawn.

The Beloved of man
Comes to walk with him into new life
And she wears the raiment of the New.
But man has sat at the looms of his consciousness
And throughout the ages has woven
The garment of his history.
When the Beloved comes and bids man arise,
Shall he leave freely the looms of his past
And the garments thereof,
And walk with her and accept her raiment,
Or will he seek to clothe her
In the garments he has woven
And seat her at his looms
And continue the weavings of the past?

The rhythms of the past are strong
Save where the soul is centered on God,
For in the presence of the Beloved
All things are made new.
The power of history
Lays a heavy hand upon the being,
Compelling his footsteps
Save where that being is one with the Beloved
In the eternal now,
For in God's presence
New creation can be born
And new history written
And a new mankind come forth.

When the dawn comes,
The sun arises
And light steals
Into the domain of shade
And the night is dispersed.
But You are beyond the dawn, Beloved,
For in You there is no darkness,
In You the sun does not rise
But is always there.
You do not stand in the twilight
Between light and shade.
You are the Oneness
And the Wholeness.
I would rise in consciousness, Beloved,
And also go beyond the dawn
To be One with You.

Let us rejoice this morning
In the love of the Beloved
Who has brought us together.
From out of time and out of space
We are brought to this point
Where we may share ourselves with each other
And in the lives of each other
Discover the many facets of the Wholeness
Which we are.
Through the ages man has sought his home;
Now he finds it as he discovers his Beloved
Within himself, within others
And in the Wholeness we share together.
Let us rejoice then this day
In the rhythms of homecoming.

I sing this morning the rhythms of laughter,
The laughter of God that moves through creation,
The laughter born of joy and of knowing
Of the perfection of it all,
For God looks forth upon creation
And knows that it is good,
And in His joy
All creation bubbles
With effervescent life and laughter,
The laughter of evolution.

God loves to laugh,
Which is why She made us,
Not to laugh at
But to laugh with
And to share the rhythms
Of Her joy.

I rise with the glory of the dawn
And receive the blessings of the new day
Which comes from golden vaults
Of new creativity.
It opens to me
The road to high adventure
And I shall not linger
But shall catch each opportunity for new life
That comes along
And in this rhythm
Shall arrive at my destiny,
The fulfillment
Of all this day has to offer.

This is the day that God has made.
It has come from Sacred hands
In beauty and perfection of opportunity
And is offered to us.
This is also the day that I shall make,
And it comes from the heights of my dreams
And the peaks of my aspirations.
May my day and His be One,
That when the sun sets,
This day will have manifested
The perfection of our united Being.

I awaken to this day
For I have opened my eyes to see it.
I awaken to love
For I open my heart to others.
I awaken to wisdom
For I open my mind to truth,
And I awaken to my Beloved
For I open myself to myself
And to all of life.
In my opening I wake to all that is
And in this wakening, a new age dawns.

ABOUT THE PUBLISHER

Lorian Press is a private, for profit business which publishes works approved by the Lorian Association. Current titles can be found on the Lorian website www.lorian.org.

The Lorian Association is a not-for-profit educational organization. Its work is to help people bring the joy, healing, and blessing of their personal spirituality into their everyday lives. This spirituality unfolds out of their unique lives and relationships to Spirit, by whatever name or in whatever form that Spirit is recognized.

For more information, go to www.lorian.org.

www.ingramcontent.com/pod-product-compliance
Lightning Source LLC
Chambersburg PA
CBHW031330040426
42443CB00005B/283